Mortality Poems

Selected and Introduced by
Veronica Esagui

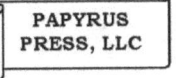

**PAPYRUS
PRESS, LLC**

West Linn, Oregon, USA

Mortality Poems
© 2024 Veronica Esagui

Library of Congress Control Number: 2024915916
ISBN 979-8-9912516-0-0

Graphics Book Designer: James M. McCracken
Editing: Veronica Esagui, John C. Fraraccio,
Genene Valleau

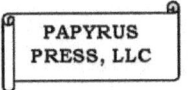

PAPYRUS
PRESS, LLC

www.veronicaesagui.com

Printed in the USA

Dedicated

In memory of

Kathleen Ruth Huff

Acknowledgements

ALEXANDRA MASON is a scholar and writer who draws on her knowledge of literature to create poems, which she also infuses with a sense of place. She is an "Oregon Legacy Author," founder of the Northwest Poets' Concord and past long-time president of Writers on the Edge.

Her poems and essays have won several awards and are widely published in journals and anthologies, including *Shakespeare Quarterly, The Oregonian, Groundwaters, 13th Moon, Sweet Smell, Oregon Stories, Seeds, Verseweavers, Love Poems, Magic Poems* and *Thresholds,* and her work is on the haiku wall in Bend, Oregon. She has written seven books, two of them volumes of award-winning poems (*Poems Along the Way* and *Lost and Found*); two novels (*The Lighthouse Ghost of Yaquina Bay* and *Shakespeare's Pipe*), and a biographical sketch of her late husband, *J. Carl Ellston of Exeter, Missouri.*

Her internationally acclaimed study of economic

metaphor has been released in a revised and expanded second edition, *Shakespeare's Money Talks*. Her most recent book is a philosophical self-help volume called *A Handbook for Love*.

alexandramasonbooks.com

Alexandra writes: *Novelist E. M. Forster is famously quoted as having said "How do I know what I think until I see what I say?" For me, poetry serves such a clarifying purpose, and ultimately a comforting purpose, as our medium, language, is through close attention ordered and magnified to a transformative lucidity. Unanswerable questions can be approached through the logic of poetry. This became especially true for me in dealing with grief, facing mortality through experience with it, articulating and exploring its philosophical and emotional aspects. I hope readers might also find insight and relief in my provisional "answers."*

AMALIE RUSH HILL is a poet, artist, and advocate for ecological, social, political and economic justice.

A prolific poet, she is working on several poetry collections. This book will be the ninth anthology containing her poetry. *The House on Prune Alley, 2016*, and *Along the Lane*, available next week, are her poetry books.

Amalie's critically acclaimed sci-fi series includes: *Ambolaja: Into the Light, Discontinuity*, and *The Shoals of Time. Z'Torr*, will be released this year.

bobhillpublishing.com

Amalie writes: *Before I learned to read, I'd scribble on paper and then tell my mother the story I wrote. After I learned to read, life suddenly became larger and more interesting. I wrote my first short story in grade school when I learned about quotations marks, and also my first poem. I write every day and am now working on my fifth novel as well as poetry, short stories and essays—it's what I do!*

ANITA BELIL, a native of New Jersey, is a retired marketing executive. Her love of poetry began in high school, and she became an avid writer during college. She endeavors to bring readers a vivid, easily relatable snapshot of everyday life through her words. She and her husband live on and work their small "hobby ranch" in Central Oregon. In addition to writing, Anita enjoys spending time with family and friends; playing folk, classical and flamenco guitar; reading; traveling; crosswords; and playing with her dogs.

Anita writes: *My poem Biorhythms is dedicated to my teachers through the decades: Dad, Ronnie, Paul, and Robin. Thank you for your everlasting patience.*

BILLIE SHULTS is a native Oregonian, born and raised in Portland. A beautiful sunset, cloud formation, tree, flower or other gifts of nature inspire Billie to let go and allow nature's divine wisdom to flow from her pen and feed her soul. She enjoys many serendipitous opportunities to share her passions through a combination of words and photography as well as following her passion as a Reiki Master. Billie is excited to be able to share her heart and art with you.

heartfelthealingtouch.wordpress.com

Award winning poet, **C. STEVEN BLUE,** stands outside the normal conventions of modern poetry: at the crossroads of poetry and music—reading and performing his work while accompanying himself with original music and hand drums. He has eight published books of his work and has been widely published in numerous literary journals and anthologies—in print, online, on radio, and on television. As an independent publisher, as well as producer and host of literary/arts events, Steven has paid it forward for years, giving countless opportunities to other creators along the way.

<u>wordsongs.com</u>

Steven writes: *"Howling Of The Moon" is a poem I wrote while pondering the aches and pains that come with getting old, losing love, and realizing the alternatives were not what I wanted—not yet!*

I wrote "Death—Yeah—Death" from a prompt in my 2017 poetry group. We were discussing poetry written from prompts and I mentioned how I felt that wisdom comes with age, and that my friend Autumn had prompted me to write a poem on that topic, which I did. The next week I presented it to the group. Then my friend Jeremy spoke up and suggested I write a poem about death. I said, "Death?" and he replied, "Death, yes death." So I wrote this epic poem.

CAROLYN MARTIN is blissfully retired in Clackamas, Oregon. She is a lover of gardening and snorkeling, feral cats and backyard birds, writing and photography. Since the only poem she wrote in high school was red-penciled "extremely maudlin," she is amazed she has continued to write.

Her poems have appeared in more than 200 journals throughout North America, Australia and the UK.

carolynmartinpoet.com

Carolyn writes: *I write for the blast of joy the process gives me and for the simmering hope that someone will read my work. My aesthetic is found in a comment by Sting, "All my life I have tried to find the truth and make it beautiful," and in Galway Kinnell's statement, "To me, poetry is somebody standing up… and saying, with as little concealment as possible, what it is for him or her to be on earth at this moment." My poems attempt to find beautiful truths as they grapple with the complexity of being on earth right now.*

CYNTHIA JACOBI lives on the Oregon Coast where she is a visual artist as well as a poet. She served on the Board of Directors for Writers on the Edge, and the Northwest Poets' Concord. She is a member of the Oregon Poetry Association and Willamette Writers. As a Friend of William Stafford, Cynthia organizes a celebration of annual birthday readings at the Newport Library.

Her poems have been published in *Verseweavers*, *Tuesday*, and most recently *The Grace of Oregon Rain*.

Cynthia writes: *Both poems are true. I was in the airplane when my Mother died. The Chemotherapy poem is about Valerie, my daughter who died January 2023. I was trimming her last wisps of hair out on the patio. It was a cool, sunny autumn day. She knew she wouldn't have time for it to grow back. I've enclosed her picture.*

DAVID RUTIEZER, was born in Skokie, Illinois, just outside Chicago, and raised in Illinois and Massachusetts. The only child of a teacher mother and a computer programmer father, he spent his childhood writing poetry and puppet shows, singing his own songs, folk dancing, and entertaining the many elders in his family, including his grandparents and great-grandparents. David's parents encouraged him from a young age to express his creativity, and to learn about the various ethnic cultures in the Chicago area.

David Rutiezer has an MFA from the Rainier Writing Workshop and TESL certification and holds a BA in Creative Writing and Theater Arts. Besides having a background in arts education, music therapy, and geriatric wellness, he offers creative writing prompts to folks with Alzheimer's and dementia to access memories and use cognition, language, and intellectual skills. He has also volunteered for several community organizations, including the Cascade Festival of African Films, Friends of William Stafford, the Oregon Holocaust Memorial, and Portland Community Dialogues. Besides being a writer, David is also a trained actor and singer and plays keyboard and ukulele. He is known for his one-man musical variety show.

creativedavid.com

David writes: *Universal emotion in poems is what I'm concerned with here, because poetry as a universal method of communication, and as a universal language of the human experience, is an aspect of poetry I'm particularly passionate about.*

EMMETT WHEATFALL resides in Portland, Oregon, where he has twice been nominated for Oregon Poet Laureate. His poetry has been published in several books, collections, anthologies, and one of them, *As Clean as a Bone*, was a 2019 Eric Hoffer Award Finalist and a da Vinci Eye award finalist. He frequently speaks about poetry and recites his own work, including during the 50th Anniversary Celebration of the March on Washington (Portland event), and as the keynote speaker at two Oregon Poetry Association's Annual Conferences. In 2020, Corban University produced a 9-part series documentary, A Brief History, that showcased Emmett's life and poetry.

emmettwheatfall.com

Emmett writes: *The Scarecrow and A Clergyman's Eulogy are poems that draw attention to the physical and metaphysical nature of life. The Scarecrow is without a soul, absent life, yet, while hoisted in the field it speaks metaphysically through its existence and silence. The Clergyman is asked to respect the death of a creature just as much as a human being.*

In these two poems are a plethora of questions that inquire about life, death, and existentialism. At my age, I often wonder about my mortality. Poetic imagery makes inquiry discernible. During such pursuit I find clarity.

FRANCIS HICKS believes the first step to living well begins with continuing to breathe. That covers the *living* part. The *well* part, he surmises, is largely how one conducts their thinking. He is fortunate to enjoy writing poems, essays and short fiction on the Oregon coast where he lives with his wife, Janet Bazemore.

His work has appeared in numerous print and on-line magazines, and anthologies including *Pine Cone Review, Emerge, Ariel Chart Magazine* and *The Way The Light Slants.* His work has been rejected by the finest magazines, including *The Sun Magazine, Rattle,* and *The New Yorker.* His debut novel *The Long Ride, Learning About Life From An Outlaw Biker* was published by Black Rose Writing in 2019. Find out more about Francis by befriending him on Facebook.

Francis writes: *In 1987 I was dealing with having abandoned a twenty-year religious obsession.*

Untitled *poem was among my first attempts to clarify (for myself) my changing mindset. For years I had allowed others to set the groundwork for my thinking. Taking personal responsibility for my own thoughts proved invigorating.*

Blackbird poem I wrote in 2021. The inevitability of dying, and the utter impossibility of knowing the experience of being dead fascinated me. I had hoped to write a short story from the idea but was satisfied with the one-page poem. It serves as a reminder to me, as one still living, to rest in things as they are.

GENIE GABRIEL is the author of 23 published books in a number of genres that incorporate her love of animals and belief in miracles. She lives and gardens on a small farm in the Pacific Northwest with a menagerie of animals who constantly teach her some of life's most valuable lessons. For excerpts from each of her books, including paranormal adventures in *The Collie Chronicles*, please visit her website.

GenieGabriel.com

Genie writes: *The recent loss of my beloved dog, Dasha, is reflected in my poem, Beyond Mortality. My other poem in this anthology, Are We Really Mortal, came to me as I have embraced being an "old woman." Knowing I am wrapping up my time here on Earth, my perception of both life and death has shifted. I don't think death is The End. Like books in a series, I believe more adventures lie beyond leaving a physical body--adventures that include loved ones who have left this physical plane before us.*

HOPE HILL is a former foster kid who writes poetry and speculative fiction. Her first poem One Touch was published in 2005 and since then she has authored the following books, *Dancing on the Ceiling, Secrets Under the Skin, Dancing in a Minefield, Dancing in a Storm, and Into the Shadow Realms - Book 1*. You can find Hope's books on Amazon.com

JEAN SHELDON has dabbled in the creative arts for much of her life. These experiments in art, poetry, mystery novels and music instilled optimism and the belief that a peaceful, united humanity is a possible and most worthy endeavor.

jeansheldon.com

JEFFREY ROSS is a retired community college English instructor who worked for 30 years at Central Arizona College. He states that his career was rewarding (and fun). Most of his teaching comprised "English 101-102," the composition courses nearly all college students complete. His book *Dr. Hill's Poet* is about a couple who falls in love through writing poems. In that book, he shows the connecting and sustaining power of heartfelt love poetry. Its characters Cassie and Sam's poems nurture them even though "society" is critical of their relationship (age differences and social status).

facebook.com/copperfieldpublishing

Jeffrey writes: *Poetry has always been interesting to me, probably because of the many courses I took in college involving Walt Whitman—the great compiler of images. I'm convinced poetry provides for a pure, distilled expression of feelings that cannot be ignored. I enjoy poetry that is short, focused, and has powerful images. I love compact, potent phrasings. I usually get my own poetic ideas from an intersection of emotions and images...if the two compliment (complement, too) each other...POEM.*

JOHN C. FRARACCIO is a New Jerseyan who knows Oregon well thanks to friends. He retired from a career negotiating contracts. With poetry he feels he negotiates English.

"It may be that the sadness that invades us and pervades our soul is due to all that we have lost before we ever possessed it. It is perhaps the regret of the best and highest part of our life that we have not lived. Perhaps we are now seeking what has died and has never been lived. ... Will the Lord gather the tears not yet shed, the harmonies suspended in the air, the songs not yet sung? Will the Lord receive my soul's weeping? I have nothing except what I have lost, except what I shall never have and what I regret. This regret and this weeping are the only thing that I could still, although unworthily, offer to my Lord. It is the better part of myself."

--*Eugenio Zolli,* Before the Dawn[1]

---

[1] Eugenio Zolli, *Before the Dawn* (San Francisco: Ignatius Press, 2008), 203 204

KATHLEEN RUTH HUFF was not a writer, much less a poet. She was a wife and mother who, out of necessity, became a successful businesswoman in the late 1960s. She ran a telephone answering service for six years while raising seven children. In 1972, however, tragedy struck the family when her firstborn son, Micheal, age eighteen, was found dead on the banks of the Sandy River in Troutdale, Oregon.

While the police ruled it a suicide, claiming Michael jumped from a nearby cliff, Kathleen fought for five years to find out what really happened to her son. In the summer of '77 she learned that he had been in a fight with an unnamed person. This person had military training and inflicted blows learned in basic training. This person knocked Michael down onto his hands and knees at the edge of the river. Then used a thick piece of tree branch to deliver a blow to the back of Michael's head. Michael fell forward, unconscious, in less than an inch of water. Kathleen later lamented, "If only he would have turned his head, he would have lived." Instead, Michael drowned in an inch of water.

Kathleen's son Matthew wrote: *My mother never shared her grief, pain, and tears in front of anyone. She kept that to herself and only wept when she was alone in her bedroom. She never knew that I heard her. It was this deep heartache that caused her to pick up a pen and write* River of Sadness. *It beautifully and painfully shares her deep sorrow. This was the only poem she wrote. She died at the age of forty-two in December of 1977.*

Kc GLOER poetic words and actions embody hope, love, intimacy and shining a light on a world that can often feel dark and overwhelming. *Nothing But Lace* is an interactive experience of passion poetry. She is presently finishing *Nothing but Love and Lace* and planning for 2025, *Nothing But the Moon, Nothing But the Sea, Nothing But Rainbows and Roses* and *Nothing But Fire and Desire.*

Lovegloriously.com

LEAH STENSON is the author of three poetry books—*Heavenly Body, The Turquoise Bee* and *Other Love Poems, Everywhere I Find Myself*—and a hybrid memoir, *Life Revised.*

She served as a regional editor of *Alive at the Center: Contemporary Poems from the Pacific Northwest* and co-editor of *Reverberations from Fukushima: 50 Japanese Poets Speak Out.* She hosts the Studio Series Poetry Reading & Open Mic in Portland.

leahstenson.com

Leah writes: *I think I became a poet because, at an early age, I realized that certain discourse was unwelcome in daily life. Poetry welcomed revelation and examination of deep and difficult truths.*

MARC JANSSEN has been writing poems since around 1980. Some people would say that was a long time but not a dinosaur. Early decrepitude has not slowed him down much; his verse can be found scattered around the world in places like *Pinyon*, *Slant*, *Cirque Journal*, *Off the Coast* and *Poetry Salzburg*, also in his book *November Reconsidered*. Marc coordinates the Salem Poetry Project that includes a weekly reading and the occasionally occurring Salem Poetry Festival. He was a nominee for Oregon Poet Laureate.

marcjanssenpoet.com

MARY E. LOWD is a prolific science-fiction and furry writer in Oregon. She has had over 200 short stories and a dozen novels published. Most of her work involves spaceships, talking animals, or both. Her work has won many awards, and she has been nominated for the Ursa Major Awards more than any other individual. You can read more of her poetry in *Some Words Burn Brightly: An Illuminated Collection of Poetry*.

marylowd.com

Mary writes*: Death is too big a subject to come at straight on. You need to circle around it, stalking it the way that it stalks you, until the whole thing turns into a dance, and when words dance, they become poetry.*

RILEE EZAGUI is a college student at the University of Oregon. She is majoring in Psychology and minoring in Art. Her plan for the future is to become a child psychologist.

Rilee writes: *I was inspired to write these poems a few years ago, based on my own personal and internal struggle dealing with depression and anger. I am glad that I was able to find a way off the dark path I was taking and I am now facing a better and brighter road.*

SHERLEY MARC started writing poetry at age 15 and had poems published in various publications sporadically. In 2005 she self-published a poetry/photo book, *Life Sat Up One Night and Caught Me*. She also compiled as co-editor a book of her grandfather's poems *When the Shadows Are Long*. For the last few years, she immersed herself in writing haiku on many topics.

She is a member of the Oregon Poetry Association and has served on the Executive Committee and as president.

Find out more about Shirley by befriending her on Facebook.

SULIMA MALZIN, who identifies as "an aging rascal & occasional writer", has been writing poetry and questioning the answers her questions have received from authority figures, since she was old enough to hold a pen. She likes to borrow Toni Morrison's explanation of writing *as a way of not just feeling, but thinking about things that are disparate, unresolved, mysterious, problematic, or just sweet.* Following the loss of her son in 2014 and a year of life-changing health challenges in 2016-17, Sulima began seriously gathering the pages she'd written over the years and putting them together in a hybrid memoir, *Arms Filled With Bittersweet*, the book in which the two poems in this anthology were first published in 2022. Never one to limit herself to a single approach when exploring creativity, this octogenarian has authored three other books bearing the titles *Words That Dance*, a collection of (mostly) poetry, first presented in 2021 with a second edition in 2023, *All In The Soup Together ... four seasons of recipes & reflections*, (for those who appreciate hearty soup and poetry on the same menu) and her latest, *Tributaries ... words of homage & gratitude*, a small volume of cento & cento-like poems paying humble tribute to the work of other poets. In addition, Sulima writes on Substack as Sulima, herSelf and on her website, sulimamalzin.net. Her work is published by Lingua Ink Books and can be purchased there, on Amazon, and at Broadway Books in Portland, Oregon.

sulimamalzin.net

SUSAN PATTERSON is an author of the heart and writer for the soul. Her work, which ranges from humorous to thoughtfully intelligent, is always quietly compelling. It has been said, her poetry is so sharp, so intricate, that it is like a Faberge egg.

Ms. Patterson has authored two books of tea poetry, *Musings with a Cuppa-The Poetry of Tea* and *Heart to Heart-Considered Sentiments for Teatime*; one book of contemporary poetry, *Unnoticed Moments*; a third book of poetry, *Passions,* is a collection of love poems. She also has a book of prose memoirs, *Tom and Irma-Memoirs of the 1950's.*

Susan Patterson has a Bachelor of Arts in English and a Master of Arts in business administration.
She and her husband, James, live a quiet life in Oregon of the United States.

EarleneGrey.com

VERONICA ESAGUI is a publisher, playwright and the critically acclaimed author of *The Scoliosis Self-Care & Resource Book* (English and Japanese), Veronica's Adventures series: *The Age of Innocence, Braving a New World, Awakening the Woman Within, Angels Among Us,* and *The Gift,* and *Aged to Perfection,* a comedy play sponsored by Fertile Grounds and performed at the Lakewood Arts Center in Lake Oswego, OR. Her poems can be found in *Moments Before Midnight, Terra Incognita,* and *Now We Heal—An Anthology of Hope* which she co-edited with Jean Sheldon. Veronica's latest publications are: *Mary Celeste—The Solved Mystery of a Ghost Ship,* a historical fiction and the poetry anthologies: *Love Poems, Magic Poems* and *Mortality Poems.*

veronicaesagui.com

Laugh

Missing your laugh today
I must water the plants
tend to the cats
refresh the sheets

Cook meals ahead to freeze.
Not even a pod of whales
I can see from our window
compensates.

The garden has never
bloomed so profusely
the colors dazzling,
vibrant.

I will try to laugh your laugh.

A Taoist Considers her Own Death

This is how it will go:
with head bent toward the ground
mind intent on clearing
the last of the skeletonweed
from the raised beds,
I shall dizzy.

The dirt will remark my fall
as no more unusual
than the drop of a pine cone.
No meteors will write
long-awaited truth through the sky.
The only shaking of the earth
will be from the steady
breaking of waves nearby.

My spark shall lodge
as a breath inhaled
in the bosoms of those I love.
All the words coiled in my mind,
ten libraries of lore,
shall empty into the

galaxy
letter by syllable
whence they came.

Lost Things

I've lost mittens and socks; as a child I lost
playmates when they moved away
I've lost weight and time,
I've lost track — I've lost unimportant things
      and I've even lost my mind
Once, at University I almost lost my purse, left it in
a classroom
      and when I went back, it was still there
I lost my flute when we moved from Nebraska to
California
There have been so many things, I've lost all
memory of them
And then the losses became people — lost to old
age and war,
      accidents and disease
My High School history teacher said every senior
class loses three people the summer after they
graduate, and he was right — three of us died that
summer: one to war, another, a scholarship winner,
drowned, and the third, I've lost the memory of who
and how
Now, the loss of old classmates and friends grows,

the numbers increase every year — all that youthful
potential lost to old age
       and cancer and suicide…
But we don't exactly lose life, it was designed to
end, mortality is sown into our genes — we'll all
fall and break; we're not superhuman even
       though as, high school seniors,
       we thought we were
That's the beauty of it — living as though we're
immortal; if we believed we were mortal, we might
simply lie down in the road and wait for Death to
come for us; but most of us don't do that — We live
on with each breath, one after another,
       not understanding that
       inhaling and exhaling
are like life and death, living and letting go;
having and losing … winning isn't the opposite of
losing, winning is ephemeral and losing goes on and
on
All we have to learn is that wisdom comes from
loss, just like each breath is only possible if it's
released, to be lost, to let it go into the wind.

I fell again

shattering my body upon the
       Earth who
waits with open arms to receive me
       and
I lie crying hot salty tears onto, into
       her body,
wetting the dry soil sending
       my blood
back where it came from, not from
       human
ancestors but from the source of all things
       here
the physical manifestation of life, of rocks
       and
motion and atoms and whales
       We
are nothing if not the planet, nothing without it,
nothing
       at all
The stars left eons ago, long since dissipated
       into
empty Cosmos, mother of Earth

      dying
from despair and grief because
      we murdered
her, daughter of Sol and the Milky Way,
      of all there is
We are ghosts now, like every extinguished
      star
only memories; but what will remember who we
were
      after the last extinction, after this final
ending?

16

Biorhythms

Some days
these six strings feel like
thin silken threads
dancing beneath my fingers
so sure, nimble and quick
sounds issue forth and
sweetly wrap around the soul
warming it, keeping it pure
and all is right in the world

Other days
these six strings feel like
thick, heavy ropes
lashing beneath my fingers
so stiff, plodding and clumsy
sounds bounce about the body
sour, and get stuck
upon the board…

Time to go back in the case

9-11-01

The day broke –
cloudless,
clear,
and carefree.

After coffee
and lollygagging
in the small, beachside rental,
we parted.

Our men, easterly,
to where golf's great hills beckoned.
We women, westerly,
towards shi-shi window fronts awaiting
to be shopped.

Ironic, how
in the Victory Garden,
hearts joyous,
bodies relaxed. . .

amongst the antiques,
platters, and planters,
challenging price tags
to real value. . .

We women learned –
our lives, and
the day
broke

Delicate Flower

I am a delicate flower
I need water to live
And maybe, a little fertilizer too
Not just when it is convenient

Mom

My mom
Long gone
Over 10 years now
I was there when she died
Peacefully
No resistance

My mom
I wouldn't be here without her
She loved me
Even through those times I doubted her

So long ago
It seems forever
To be in her presence
Yet I still feel her essence
It is a part of me

People ask me about my family
My family tree has broken branches
Some were grafted
Some never lasted

Some grew new homes, in new places
Like leaves blowing in the wind
Separated from source
Feeling no remorse
Standing tall
Greeting the fall
Fading into the season
Waiting for a reason
To spring into a burst of glory
Creating an umbrella of love
To remember
Where I came from
And where I will go
After the summer sun's glow
Fades into a starry nighttime show

I will remember
Peacefully
Without resistance
The lessons of
Mother
Nature
And all her essence

28

Death—Yeah—Death
(excerpt #2)

Is there really life after death,
Or is it just death,
You know, that thing you think so much about?
Well, maybe not so much, but sometimes,
Because it's inevitable.
It's what we are all headed for.

So, Death, yeah, Death
Is a part of life
We all have to face.
It doesn't leave any of us
Behind.

DEATH!
Death and destruction!
Regression!
Evolution!
Ashes to Ashes!

I often say life
Is like a car engine.

We're just wearing out
A little bit at a time.
Eventually the valves'll freeze,
Or you'll crack your head (gasket),
And eventually you'll die
. . . Because you just wear out!

I often think about death now,
But I think about it
In the sense of time.
Time is so important.
When I was young,
Time seemed like forever.

You know, when you're young
You feel invincible,
Like you can do anything;
And, pretty much, you can.
And you also have the energy to do it!

As you grow older,
You realize that time is fleeting.
Time moves pretty fast,
And the older you get,

The faster it seems to go.
And that's rough, sometimes,
Because you want it to just
—Slow down!
So you can get all the things done
You want to do.

So, mostly, what I think about
When I think about death,
Is how much time
Do I have left?

But who knows . . . where the time goes,
As the grass grows,
And the poems compose?

So, Death, yeah, Death.
Something we all have
To look forward to.
It doesn't
Leave any of us behind.
Cuts to the core.
Comes for us all.
When it knocks on your door,
You must heed the call.

Death, yeah, Death.
I hope it waits long enough
For me to get some things done.
Life can be rough.
Time won't slow down.
I'll take it when it comes.
Death, yeah, Death
Is just a part of life.

Howling Of The Moon

I saw it in your eyes once,
not so long ago.
I felt it when you smiled at me
with that old familiar glow.

But the magic seems so rare now
in the autumn of my years.
The things that used to tingle inside
can now bring me to tears.

Oh, the long and cloudy years,
the range of which ran broad,
dissolve into the aches and pains
that now make me feel flawed.

I've slipped . . . and fallen down;
don't know if I can get back up
to feel again, what I felt back then,
when you filled my loving cup.

Are all my love songs written?
Is this the last hurrah?
Will I never again be smitten
by the beauty that I saw?

Are all my love songs written?
Did it all just end so soon?
Will I ever again feel the passion
or the howling of the moon?

I felt it in the way you moved
in the once again so new.
The moon was full, your curves were round,
oh how your fancy flew.

But the flying is less frequent
and the motivation's mild.
The things that used to drive me mad
no longer are so wild.

I've settled into the distance
and hung my tears to dry.
Now all I have is a vague resistance
to call my dreams and try.

Are all my love songs written?
Is this the last hurrah?
Will I never again be smitten
by the beauty that I saw?

Are all my love songs written?
Did it all just end too soon?
Will I ever again feel the passion
or the howling of the moon?

Oh, the small and whispered wonders
that barely recall my youth;
the forget me nots that I forgot
in all the tangled truth.

And it's a melancholy madness
      that I've stumbled.
It now creates this sadness
      and I'm crumbled.

In a lifetime of Love's passioned memories
and heartfelt,
      often missed,
            discoveries,

I truly do admit
      that I am humbled.

Are all my love songs written?
Is this the last hurrah?
Will I never again be smitten
by the beauty that I saw?

Are all my love songs written?
Did it all just end too soon?
Will I ever again feel the passion
or the howling of the moon?

Casualty

Route 26 through the Coast Range to
Seaside, Oregon

Miles of mute taillights
and a woman crushed beneath
a logging truck.
Her soul clicks off
her Honda's seatbelt
and rises through
fog-wet firs,
confounded by the ruckus
she's stirred up.
She shouts apologies
to the drivers cursing
the delay, tries
to explain how her mind,
mangling tears with regret,
swerved toward
the New Jersey grave
where her mother's ashes
stir beneath the autumn sun.
That's where I was, she cries
frantically to campers/cars/SUVs;

over flares of aggravation and prayers.
That's where I was,
she insists, *shouting*
words I never said.
My mother's dead.
Lanes blurred.

Afterwards,
when the fireplace and cups
of tea soothed the anxiety
of the five-hour stall,
we still don't know
the how or who.
A flannel shirt, jogging
to the barricades,
reported back to lanes
of windows rolling down:
woman dead/gas spill/
unpredictable delays.
By the time we eased
through, nothing's left
but road-shine, shattered trees,
and curiosity about
a woman someone loved.

Tonight's news? Mute.
What we hear—and hearing
is all we can do—
Western gulls flapping
past our balcony,
relentless waves scouring
the shore, and—
if we lean in close enough —
predictable fog shrouding
a sun straining to set.

(Formerly published in *Panoplyzine*)
© 2022 Carolyn Martin

To a Dear Friend Dealing with Acute Anxiety

Your call yesterday was a relief.
Two good days, you said. Back pain eased,
heart settled down, and the doe you've tracked
through flower beds and trees befriended you.
A spirit guide, I laughed, and you agreed.
Now, you share, you're lost in a forest of grief—
family, friends, colleagues gone—and losses
          devastate.
I hesitate to tell you this for it's mine to own:
I've held grief in my arms and walked it up
and down city streets. I've stood at gravesides
as it crumbled to the ground. I've learned
from betrayal and hurt, cruelty and loss,
there is no grief like ours and earth is rich with it.
So what to do, dear friend, when your grief
          consumes?
Go outside and find your guide. She's waiting for
          you.
She'll probably advise that grief is a mystery
that can't solve itself. Ask her how to befriend
emptiness until the joy chasing you catches up.
Ask her to confirm it takes eternities to fill voids

and, in all that space and time, blessings are yours
        to give.
If you listen deeper than you thought you could,
you might hear that love is another name for grief.

Previously published in *Deal Jam.*

Mercy for My Mother/Regrets for My Late Arrival

In another time, you might have floated
on a burial pyre into a dark fjord
A proud and honored princess
of a wandering tribe
You left as a candle flame
slow snuffed lacking oxygen
Your passage eased by morphia
bitter drops under the tongue
Gone were green cylinders and tubing
cups, straws, swabs, the to-do list
Your body had been rolled and zipped
into the pre-planned biodegradable bag
The mattress had been washed
rolled and zipped, tossed into a truck
A skeleton bed frame of bare wires
naked coiled springs exposed
Threw shadows of connecting
circles and spirals and crosses
Shaped by your final repose
knee crank up, head raised

© 2012 Cynthia Jacobi

Chemotherapy – Week 8

Clumps of falling hair clot the brush
Don't throw it away, she says
Put it over there
Over there in that shrub
For the nesting birds
Next spring

Waiting in the PCC Parking Lot for the Cars to Clear

The parking lot though enlarged
is still inadequate for the number of cars
and trapped in my parking place
I spend the elongated minutes
noticing plants in their sunken beds,
the angles of brick, a woman's dark hair
contoured by afternoon light,
a stray dried leaf, a student walking past.

When my mother and I were trapped years ago in
the condo for almost a week
during a big ice storm, I imagined two spiders
and how, when one spider finds the other's corner,
one will end up eaten by the other
with only its spindly legs left behind,
one leg still pulsing with the same energy
it'd had in life. And how everything that week
felt swollen and claustrophobic.
My mom's dressers of drawers seemed to be
watching me and brown splotches expanded on
the bananas in the basket on the kitchen counter

and my grandparents' old clock that my mom
never could get rid of still didn't work
sitting on my grandparents' old piano
that still no longer played beneath their big old
painting of European houses along a river with
some big cathedral looming in the background.
The place seemed to sink into itself.
On the fourth day of the lock in I couldn't stand it
any more and I blew up at my mother.

And now, she isn't here at all, she's just gone
and the radio blares another mass shooting
and now I can finally pull out of my parking place
and I obsess again about my always low bank
account, again a prisoner to life's arithmetic,
all the way to the pizza place
where I settle for the one-trip salad bar
and the balloon man twists happiness into
two brothers who were fighting when I came in
and the 1980s music takes me back to high school
and being a passenger in my parents' car
when a song was all it took to be free.

In the West (March 1987)

I had never seen red earth with deep green pines etched in white snow.

I drove over the pass and then down into Laramie, Wyoming. Suddenly, I was in the west, driving all the way from Mt. Vernon, Iowa, where I'd been kicked out of college, to Portland, Oregon, where my mom had moved in the meantime, abandoning me. From Chicago, land of straight streets divided by occasional diagonals, stretching into the flat horizon, a city of blocks into suburbs. I'd visited California and Oregon via plane. On the way to Oregon with my mom, we'd descended into Salt Lake City, marveling at multilayered cliffs. But I had never driven into the mountains.

I was 18 and didn't think about politics. The ranches on either side with snow-capped mountains towering above them, the people in cowboy hats and jeans, felt exciting and patriotic. I listened to the only radio stations whose signal came in: country. Someone named Earl Thomas Conley lamenting: Love Don't Care (Whose Heart it Breaks). I listened and sang along.

My mom hadn't believed me when I told her. And Ichiro, my foreign-exchange roommate from Tokyo had asked "Do you know what people are saying about you?" As I made my way west, I surely drove past the exact spot where, 13 years later, a young man the age I was now would hang beaten, bloodied and burned from a fencepost outside one of those ranches beneath those same imposing mountains.

For being gay. Like me.

Scarecrow

Yell out loud whenever needed
Only remember, scarecrow is listening
Underneath balmy sky

Seed sown is not scarecrow sustenance
Ontologically, a truism
Languid stands the tepid scarecrow
Vociferously you yell on its behalf
Eureka!

Insanely satisfying that epiphany
To scarecrow's masked delight

© 2024 Emmett Wheatfall

A Clergyman's Eulogy

So, you're nihilistic
Doesn't a bird deserve burial
It too shares the same Creator

With eyes shut
Can't you sing a hymn
At least fake a prayer

After passing from this life
With eyes open
A clergyman's eulogy

Will offer you up to Heaven
As much as the earth
Offers up a bird

Art by: Tim Hicks

Untitled

We too shall die someday.
And when we do what will they say?
That we were kind and true and clean?
Or that our actions harsh and mean?
Or maybe something in between.

No one can know what will be said
When we too are laid down dead.
But in the time from now 'til then
No one can cause what will have been
Except for us, whose life we spend.

Though others make their pitch to us,
Of how to live, of whom to trust,
If we should shoot with faulty aim
There is no one should take the blame
The consequences we must claim.

For though life is a mystery
And we seek help from those we see
It's still our job to find our way.
To pilot through dark skies and gray,
To take us to our final day.

And on that day when we are dead,
And our histories are read,
Who cares what those around shall say?
If praise abounds or critics bray.
We won't care from where we lay.

It's how we live right now that counts.
With all the things we must surmount.
Each one must find what brings them joy
And let no one by clever ploy
Take from them this right of choice.

Art by: Tim Hicks

Just Sleep

I sat in meditation formation for half an hour and found lack. No sense of direction. A hollow space for thoughts to parade.

But this is not the subject.

The lede is *death.*

The theme experience: of death awake, of death alert, of death aware. Coming to this space took no effort, no practice—only the realization of sameness.

Life is never the same.

But, death is.

Who or what could know except the consciousness of the unconscious—the alert, awake, astute experience of a realm no one definitively writes about?

No one can.

But, the blackbird *told me.*

"Let go," it said. "Give your anxiety a rest. It doesn't serve you anymore."

And so, I let go.

And listened. And pondered.

The bird was correct; my anxiety no longer served

to keep me safe from all the real and imagined pitfalls of *living.*

But, awake I was: feeling, experiencing, collecting data moment by moment, observing that nothing changed.

I wondered *why?*

In life everything changes. Stasis was the clue that lit the light that gave me understanding. This was death, from which no escape existed.

But what am I to do?

"Just sleep," the blackbird said. "Just sleep."

© 2021 Francis Hicks

Beyond Mortality

The losses bruise my soul
and take their toll
on the life I could be living.

Others who know their own grief
and offer comfort
only confirm my desire
to curl into a terrified ball
and hide behind a façade
of philosophical murmurings
and stoic humor.

For if I open my heart
and share my grief
will I be forever shattered
into so many pieces
there will be nothing
to put back together?

Or is sharing our grief and brokenness
the way to move beyond mortality?
The way to truly heal the grief of all and

together create something far more beautiful
than what we could achieve on our own?

© 2024 Genie Gabriel

Are We Really Mortal?

If we truly live forever,
as some believe,
Are we really mortal?

For how can you be mortal
and immortal at the same time?

Do we simply change physical bodies
and come back as someone new?
Is that why someone can see their parent
in the face of their grandchild?

Or if we build a legend
that is carried on by our children
and their children
and their children's children
Have we become immortal
through that legend?

Possibilities, my friend.
What do you believe?

© 2024 Genie Gabriel

Death Can Wait

Mortality hits different
When you grow up
Expecting to die
Future becomes
A foreign language
You've forgotten
How to speak
Life exists in past & present
The only thing
You remember about the future
It was never promised
I will die someday
But death's embrace
Can wait

© 2024 Hope Hill

I Woke up Dying

It was an august morning
I'll never forget
When I woke up dying.
Ten years later
I still remember how it felt
It hurt to move
It hurt to not move
It hurt to breathe
I limped to the hospital
Leaning on my partner
Blinking in and out of consciousness
Knowing if I fell I'd die
It took everything I had
To make it five blocks
I walked into the ER
The doctor told me
I had a kidney infection
Asked me to stay for observation
Just as a precaution
I was wheeled to the surgical ward
Told they had no other beds
For three days they treated me

And nothing more was said
I'd later learn both kidneys failed
And I'd gone septic
It took five years
For my kidneys to recover
But I'll never forget
How close I came to dying

It's Not Over

We watch the sky
sensing that even a force
as intense as the sun
will someday transform.
Understanding that it is the nature
of energy to change.
But intellect, or perhaps fear,
leads us down an awkward path
seeking immortality for this
temporary form.
Yet, as with every star,
we will change,
and the transformation
will be breathtaking.

© 2024 Jean Sheldon

Of Time

Tick
A lifetime
The blink of an eye.

What tricks these
passing seconds play.
Tick

Long when waiting
but a year,
a decade,
a lifetime,
here and gone.

Tick
No apology.
No remorse.
Only another soft
Tick.

Those Golden Years Coax

Oh, those Golden Years coax like soothing lovers,
whispering sweet and measured phrases: retirement
homes ... European travel ... pickleball ... noon
buffet ... loving grandkids ...

(Maybe all true for you, maybe not.)

The words are fleeting and delusional in any sad
context.

Mortality lurches discreetly behind the shadows ... a
dark, calculating companion who cannot be ignored
... a figurine colossus, relentless and direct.

Smiling providers and franchised clinics are
waiting, despite the gym and your morning walks.

Hospitals have your name etched in an unforgiving
... and permanent ...
stone-cold ledger ....

Knee replacement, Afib, failing eyesight, arthritis,

bypass ... obesity, diabetes ... none are illusions.
Hospice care beckons, just a few Thanksgiving
dinners distant.

Perhaps five happy years remain for you—even ten
or twenty.
But the best-paid retirement planner cannot avoid
the final tax, the terminal payment ...

Mortality never cares who is naughty or nice.

Yes, we are irrevocably booked on the closure
cruise ... the destination fixed and non-negotiable.

Golden Years coax like soothing lovers, whispering
sweet phrases. But Mortality Conquers All.

When the Time Comes

When the time comes...
You know, the dark time, closing time...Mortality's
final waltz...

What will I consider? Sketchy lists of projects
incomplete ? Shameful acts I can't deny? Bad
decisions? The gigs I avoided?

No.

Just one thing, one event, one moment—
inadequacy's capstone.

A measure of rests.

You see...
I never told you (sweetest of all souls and
symphonies) the truth about those feelings...
I believed I was respectful of your life, your
presence, your happiness....

But the opposite is true...
Mortality now highlights my cowardice...
And will quiet the music...
And the simplest non-disclosure, a forgotten song
Will haunt my eternity....
I suppose I thought I'd sing it to you someday. Too late.

The waltz moves in 3/4 time.
I could only muster 7/8.

The Star Goes Out

I hope to be afforded the pleasure of the view
       of a near-Winter's moonless twilight
       on the beach
       at low tide
       the surf more at rest
       despite the westerly breeze
The Sun had set not long before
       leaving a shrinking pastel streak
       but no clouds
       and any stars were burgeoning at best
I was told to look for a passing airliner
       whose lights did not blink
       made no sound
       did not change course
       left no contrail
And there it was
       no shooting star this
       but only one light that (sure enough)
           did not blink
           and (so I was told)
           reflected only the hidden Sun
       made no sound

easterly bearing
low on the horizon
straight
over the darkened summer homes
    and dimmed streetlamps
towards me
passing directly overhead
heading out to sea
steady as it went
winking out
    because (so I was told)
    it had entered our Earth's shadow
I stayed awhile
Not truly expecting an encore
But I had seen enough to last at least
    well
    when the time comes
I hope to be afforded the pleasure of the view
    of Home

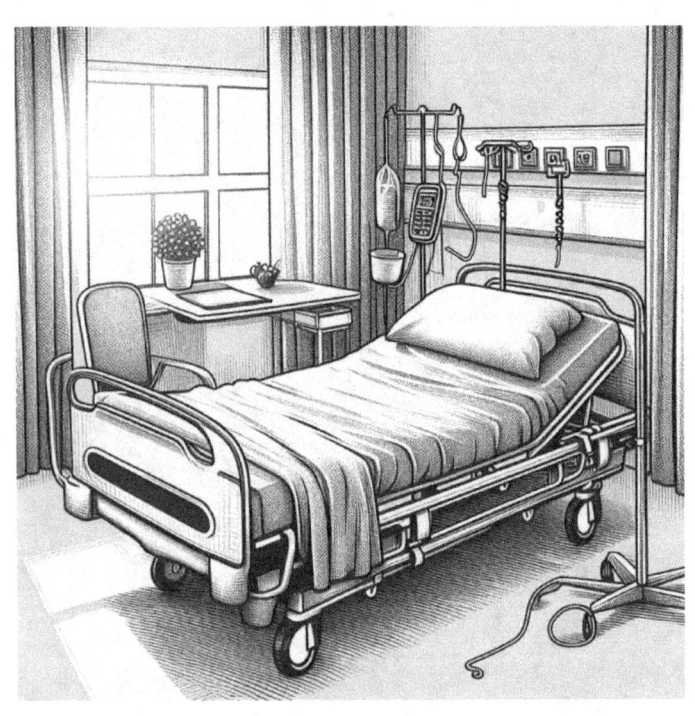

Prognoses

0

I focus on dots
The chart tells me nothing more
My specialist knows

I

My blinds are drawn closed
I know the Sun's behind clouds
The birds tell me so

II

The IV drip *ticks*
My only true sense of time
That I can't measure

III

Family and friends
Stop share hide withdraw exit
I hear one blessing

IV

I sleep too easy
Can't tell distractions apart
Nothing more to say

River of Sadness

(In Memory of her son, John Michael Huff, II)

On a bright sunny afternoon,
Three boys down the river came soon
Upon a young man motionless.
Oh, River of Sadness!

The police, siren screaming, came to see,
Down a steep trail and round many a tree,
Finally to view a wasted youthfulness.
Oh, River of Sadness!

The river patrol would work this day.
Up the river the boat sped on its way
To bring out the body of lifelessness.
Oh, Great River of Sadness!

Miles away a phone was ringing
In a home where a family was laughing
The caller's words filled the father with
dreadfulness.
Oh, River of Deep Sadness!

The deputy coroner did not falter.
He told of large rocks and shallow water.
A suicide he said in all kindness.
Oh, River of Sadness.

He led them to a room at the end of a hall
Opened the door and there they saw
Their son – his father's name and likeness.
Oh, River of Sadness!

With heads bowed in grief and hearts breaking,
A positive identification they were making
As they stood hand in hand motionless
Oh River, River of Great Sadness!

With a crushing grief the mother's heart bled
For her firstborn child was dead.
She prayed to God her child to bless.
Oh, River of Eternal Sadness!

Lord, give us the words to ease the children's tears
When the news they must hear
Let us explain their brother's eternal happiness
Oh, River of So Much Sadness!

God gave the mother a special grace
A gentle smile he placed on her face
As a priest told of their son's Eternalness
Oh, River of Sadness.

Now the parents have just one prayer.
To find out what happened out there.
In a cove beside the water so restless
Oh, River of Sadness, River of Sadness.

At Rest

When the sun is setting
I reach for your hand
The silence has come
God has called you home

Til death do us part
Means nothing at all
For even in death
You'll stay in my heart

I know you'll be there
Every night the sun sets
Every single evening
In my soul, your hand will rest

You will be there to guide me
To welcome me home
When my time appears
Across the horizon we'll roam

Joining you there
At last to be free
No more worries
Of what is to be

Free to love
Letting everything go
Where all that is left
Is the love we had known

So goodbye my darling
Find your happiness there
Among all the angels
So gentle with care

Your spirit now cleansed
Your torment at an end
Run in the rainbows
Rest in the clouds

At peace now forever
Forever is now

© 2024 Kc Gloer

Fading

Oh weary am I
As my soul softly weeps
Amidst this fog-lit eve
Tears fading into mist
Sadness abounds
On this dreary night
Where cries for help
Are lost in the wind
Where a broken heart
Will never mend
Where loneliness
Is more comfort than a friend
Is this how it is supposed to end?

Dance of the Trees

I'm waiting for the wild cherries
to tango again like they did last fall
when they dipped and swayed,
trunks wound around one another,
leaves from golden tresses
shimmying to the ground.

I wish the season would linger, forestall
winter winds that strip branches bare,
snow that stills the dance, before
limbs downed by age and ice
are consigned to winter fires.

Let's renounce the warmth of the stove
where we've been firmly planted
watching wood go up in smoke,
shake ourselves loose,
cascade like powdered snow
from the boughs of wind-bent firs.

© 2020 Leah Stenson

MEMORIAL TRIBUTES

Celebrate their life with our community.

Celia Funk
July 23, 1941 – July 8, 2024

Celia Ann Funk, widow of Wilbur Earl Funk, and mother of Matthew Funk and Daniela Laureen Funk and Nicholas Matthew Funk, passed away after suffering from Alzheimer's disease for many years, on Monday, July 8, 2024, at Parkview Memory Care facility in SE Portland, at the age of 81. She and Wilbur shared over 40 years of marriage, music, and laughter together while on Earth, may this now continue infinitely in heaven, accompanied by the angels and Celia's beautiful clouds.

Per Celia's request, there will be no memorial service of any kind; she will join Wilbur in his niche at Willamette National Cemetery.

Please sign the online guest book at www.oregonlive.com/obits

Patricia Purdy
May 27, 1937 – July 13, 2024

Pat Purdy of Portland, Ore., died peacefully at her home, surrounded by family, on July 13 at the age of 87.

Pat was born on May 27, 1937 in Portland, Ore., to Joseph and Barbara Manning. A lifelong Oregonian, she graduated from Washington High School in 1955. In 1956 she married Sam Purdy, Jr., who preceded her in death in 2004. Together they raised two children, Jim (Tim) and Lisa. She worked as an Executive Assistant and HR Manager for Fine Arts Engraving for many years. Pat maintained an active schedule after retirement, traveling, volunteering, walking and participating in a wide variety of activities with a large circle of dear friends. Her family will remember and miss her love, her competitive nature when playing games, and of course, her biscuits. Pat is survived by her children Jim (Kimberly) and Erin (Jay), her sister Marilyn Sciacca (Myrna), Erik (wife Rachel), partner Caitlin), Stephen (wife Susie), Erik (wife Rachel), and great-grandchildren Theo and Calvin. She will be reunited with Sam at Willamette National Cemetery.

Please sign the online guest book at www.oregonlive.com/obits

Thomas Johnston
July 27, 1942 – July 12, 2024

Thomas Johnston passed away unexpectedly but peacefully on July 12, from July 27, 1942 in Portland, Tom was the son of Alexander and Anna Johnston. He formed his early years in the Portland area graduating from Wilson High School. After graduating, he began his service in the US Navy. Tom earned a BS degree in Business/Accounting from Portland State University. He immediately moved to southern California to start a 25-year career including as Western Regional CFO for Merrill Lynch and owner/broker for Realty Executives/NorthStar Financial. In addition to his busy work schedule, Tom attended the police academy of the LA Police Department and became a reserve officer serving from 1975-1997 working night shifts in South Central, Los Angeles. When he "retired" in 2010 from the real estate business and returned to Portland and assumed the position of... for The Madeleine Catholic Church until his... life being a confirmed bachelor... life. They married in...

in Manhattan Beach and Palm Springs...

Golda F. Fabian
May 14, 1923 – July 4, 2024

Golda Faye Fabian passed away on July 4, 2024 at the Dancer's home in Tualatin, Ore. Her daughter, Betty Blain, and Golda's niece, Teri Loop, were by her side when she took her last breath. Golda was born in McMinnville, Ore., in Harry and Agnes Hammerli in 1923.

She is survived by her son, Mes schoitingson, daughter Betty Blain, stepdaughter Kristin Garrett and step-daughter Antonia (Tom) Kremmel. She was predeceased by a son, Make Allan Whitenighton, and her husband, Andy Fabian.

Golda supported her family as a bookkeeper until she retired to know her mid-eighties. Those who knew her said that she died on the 4th of July. Interestingly, she joined the Women's Marine Corps during the war and was an active member of the Rose City Chapter of the Woman Marines Association up until her death.

Cremation services will be held at the Willamette National Cemetery on July 30, 2024, at 2 p.m. Following the service, friends and family will gather to celebrate her life at the Monarch Hotel.

In lieu of flowers, the family suggests that a donation be made to The Susan G. Komen Foundation (T2T.org) or The Shriners Hospital Tutorial in Portland, Ore., where she was treated for polio when she was a child.

Please sign the online guest book at www.oregonlive.com/obits

Thomas Grinnell
Dec. 2, 1942 – July 14, 2024

Margaret B. Robnett
May 27, 1938 – June 23, 2024

Margaret was born in Corvallis, Ore., to parents Pete and Audrey Blackstone. She attended Corvallis High School and played saxophone. While still in high school, she played cello with the Oregon State University orchestra. Margaret attended Oregon State University where she met her future husband James Robnett. They were married on... for a short time... settled in Happy... where they raised... Margaret was a beloved... community... notably at Kaiser Sunnyside Hospital for over 30 years. Margaret was preceded in death by her husband, Jan... sister, Nancy Hawkins and brother-in-law, Hank Hopkins (Cathy) and two granddaughters. She is survived by her... Robnett... of Santa Rosa, Calif...

Family and Friends

My grandfather died in the garage
of carbon monoxide from his new Cadillac.

My grandmother died alone in the next room
overcome by the fumes.

A one-year-old cousin died never having
taken a stride, a hole in his heart.

As for me, young, learning to run,
death kept on coming.

My other grandmother died of a stroke
I am told, but she was old.

My father died on New Year's Day
of a heart attack, his class papers graded
ready to hand back.

His youngest brother died of a stroke,
although he never smoked.

His middle brother, the family joker,
died after months in a coma.

My husband's father died of emphysema,
railing and wheezing, nowhere to hide.

His wife died at home,
a nurse and a neighbor at her side.

One cousin died of breast cancer,
avoidable perhaps, due to a relapse.

Another cousin died alone, decomposing
for days in a Bronx apartment.

One aunt died of a heart attack, stuffed
with Thanksgiving turkey, flat on her back.

Another aunt died surrounded by lovely things;
then the nursing home staff stole her wedding ring.

This summer, a friend died, his car rolling over,
plunging into a ravine from the road's soft shoulder.

A friend's son died of a drug overdose
in a field, a fallow yield.

Still, another friend died, an Aikido black belt
in his prime, of liver cancer, before his time.

Another from the tiny cut of a knife,
leaving behind a child and wife.

Another on the battlefield in war so he won't
be coming home anymore.

My husband wants to die in our garden
on a sunny summer day eating lemon sorbet.

If I must die, I want to be in bed,
my daughters by my side stroking my head.

Book of Cold Water

Ruth Orr died.
Breath and spirit crossed between upper and lower plates,
Slipped silently out of chasmed dry lips,
Tongue relaxed at the back of her mouth
As if resting after a long walk.
Gray hair, probably in curls, wispy.
Eyes closed, head pushed back into sterile pillows,
Consciousness escaping
And the pain of her husband's death just two days before.
And though there was relief, there was surprise, a sudden realization
Like the first moments of labor, when she realized it was time
She knew it was time, and there was no time.
There are words to be said.
There are things left to do.
Not important things, but laundry, clothes to be put on,
Friends to be visited, children.
Grandchildren, great grandchildren to be touched...

Perhaps that Benny Goodman record...
Cold water drawn directly from the tap;
Let slide down a parched throat, the taste and the
coolness.

Coolness, like the feeling of the Klamath
across her young thirty year old feet, under the
shade of hills and trees of heaven, gnats alight in the
slanting rays of the sun, capture it for a moment and
relinquish it to the safe keeping of shadows and
onrushing night, the soft breath of river weeds
brushing her ankles, and double clicks of dragonfly
wings, the smooth movements of herons taking
flight one last time, the cackle of a crow;
blackberries, picked, wait in a bucket to become
tomorrow's cobbler; a nearby rumble of the old
truck's engine and voices "it's time to go, it's time to
go."

There is no hurry, no panic
Just surprise and knowledge that in this last moment
Half gone now that the breath has left.
This last moment of relaxation is all there is.
All that is left
And time, not clocks and watches, but real time

Gone.

Surprise.

Relief.

Salem January V

You can walk to the window, look out over the
street:
Industrial glass of the Revenue Building or of the
North Mall Office Building,
The stately tall windows of the Reed Opera House's
upper floors,
Apartments of Salmon Run,
Or in the Ram the windows that blink at the
abandoned patio.
It is the same
Dark outside
Your image looking back.
What does it see?
A jacket, a scarf
Longing.
Someone a little older than yesterday;
A little older than last week.

The Paradox of Linearity

Someday nothing will pass before my eyes
No touches will startle my senses
The spark igniting my mind will die
My experience of this world will have ended

But these lines are immortal
Lasting on and on
A string plucked in the universe
Forever resonating, on and on
For once the words are written
They're always written
(Forget forgotten)
(It only means something to you—
—inside your mind)
Out here, everything that happens
Has forever happened
And in the past is always
—will always be—
Happening

Am I the moment happening?
Or am I the observer of moments?
Am I immortal (like my words)
Or intrinsically transient?

Always alive
—once happened
Always happening—
Or always dying?
Each moment, passing from one self
To the next?

Am I the same author who started
Writing this poem
Only moments
Ago?

The Ultimate, Unsolvable Puzzle

Death is a puzzle
My mind wants to wrestle
Until all the pieces fall into place
And I'm no longer scared
—petrified, horrified, frozen—
By the idea of less than darkness
Not even a quantum trace
(Just barely enough
To signify to the world:
You are observed)
Not even that
Not
Even

My Black, Pink, and Red Emotions

Part I

When it's late at night
and my mind starts to wander
I can no longer fight the demons away.

They speak to me in their cold black words
and cause me to be swept into sadness
No strength, no control,
nothing to block them out.

I can feel the blackened words
battle their way into my soul
slowly killing me from the inside out.

I know what is happening,
but I have no way to stop them.
I just fall into their black abyss,
with no way out, and no hope for release.

© 2022 Rilee Ezagui

Part II

Joy, euphoric, what's the difference?
Nothing
Just different pink drugs
Coursing through my veins
making me crave more.

I thrive off the idea
when I get to take my next dose
Get to feel the pink, bubbly, joy
rain over me,
once again.
I wish I could collect it
like butterflies,
able to keep the feeling
with me, forever.

At last,
I can't,
so forever I will be chasing
the pink joyful
butterfly's toxic air.

© 2022 Rilee Ezagui

Part III

Anger is a unique feeling
when my face becomes red
and my mind begins to plot
horrendous things.

The rage begins to create a redden key
A key releases all the dangerous thoughts
and words I have been taught to lock away.

I fight the feeling
trying to swallow it
like a big red pill
slowly and painfully choking me.

A volcano is about to explode
its red-hot lava over the town
and kill all that it touches.

I stab the beast with the red fur
until the last drop of blood
has bled out
and the feeling slowly begins to subside.

Too Beautiful

The look of your face surveying the ocean
and the tiny creatures scurrying in the sand,
creating a map for you to follow down the shore.
The wonder of your eyes following the birds, now
gobbled up by low lying fog, until surfacing
from the depths, with silver, slippery fish
in engorged gullets—an unimaginable fullness.

Tromping through ferns, leaves, sticks, vines
and tree roots that threaten to throw you down
headfirst into mucky underbrush, you pause,
listening for the call of the red-winged blackbird.
But all is silent, while a mouse, winking at the light,
follows a hawk circling his underground nest,
preparing to run or dive into hopeful safety.

Climbing rocks against the sun, foreboding
written on their surfaces, you move higher
up the cliffs over black, hardened ash.
This once impenetrable barrier of flowing lava
is now open to your command as a vast field
to be explored of unfamiliar shapes and textures,
until reaching the steam-filled crater, still bubbling.

A no-man's land, a place for a daring spider or fly,
or hard-shelled creatures taking their chances,
wobbling on the brink of eternity into sudden death.
A wayward bird swoops closely singeing its wing,
fluttering off with ungainly momentum, lopsided.
And you, tottering at the edge, turn too quickly,
Knowing you were too beautiful for this world.

Unravel My Heart

As if pulling on a thread that unravels my heart,
the long, droning sound of the train whistle haunts
me through the night, wanders through my dreams,
and awakens me to the reality—you are gone.

What explanation is needed? What is wanted?
How can what once was, no longer exist?
What was once felt, can no longer be touched;
What was once animated, no longer breathes.

Why is this wrenching mystery a burden,
a case to be solved, a puzzle to finish?
Where are the lost pieces that linger so
deeply in my conscious thought—still.

Yes, stillness is the medicine, the succor
that will mend this being of mine, glue
it back together in some semblance of
realness—cohesive, strong, indestructible.

Yet the train comes again, and again, and
again as it rolls through the countryside,
saying I have come to remind you, nudge
you, the one who needs to remember —

That night, before all was changed, became
unreal, lost, unbearable, waiting for some
thing, someone, some arbitrary word of hope,
of love, of peace, of kindness, of sanctuary.

The Winter My Mother Died

I felt cold all the time

cold unlike any other I had ever known
as if an icicle loosened from a steep roof
had plunged dead center into my belly
during that eternal moment I waited
for her breath to return.

I wanted to believe in warmth

tried to imagine lifting my face to the sun,
yearned to wake and find myself in a garden
in the long light of a summer evening.
But flowers cannot bloom before their buds
have formed and buds are nothing until
the ice around dormant roots has melted
into the warming earth.

I could only trust that spring would come

© 2022 Sulima Malzin

Ready, or Not

I am not ready to die
But I am learning to trust death
As I have trusted life.
I am moving
Toward a new freedom.

> May Sarton
> *Gestalt at 60*

> *If I ever die, I'd like it to be*
> *in the evening. That way, I'll have*
> *all the dark to go with me, and no one*
> *will see how I begin to hobble along.*
>> William Stafford
>> *Things I Learned Last Week*

Since I could not stop for Death
He kindly stopped for me ...
The carriage held but just Ourselves
And Immortality.

> Emily Dickinson
> *Because I could not stop for Death*

I am not ready to die either, but I have learned to trust the process of continuation, to love the changing seasons and to accept that there is one for every thing. So I suppose that evening would be a good time for death to come for me; ideally at sunset, after a day rich with beauty and conversation, human touch and good food.

That I wouldn't feel cheated, especially if I were to glance up just in time to see the vehicle from which it beckoned careening without notice around the corner.

I don't think about death very much …. that is, I don't focus or perseverate or even give it the time of day with any regularity. Death in the abstract can be intriguing, even seductive. Dying, on the other hand, is a challenge. Dying is the messy part, the painful, uncertain, confusing part …. the part that can stumble and drag on beyond all expectation, with no regard for those who will be left. I myself don't mind uncertainty. I can think of worse things.

In my imagination I'd like to be the one who, when gently asked about what appears to be less than perfect health, might reply with a smile, *Well yes, I'm living with a situation they say is terminal.* I like that idea because it makes time for *Goodbyes*. But who's to say how it will be? The only certainty is death itself. How the dying will occur and how long it will take remains to be seen.

Tomorrow perhaps I will consider whether thinking about it makes me more ready, or not. In this moment a small brown wren is pecking her way across my window ledge and for now I will give her my full attention.

The Widow

She would feel the pain of her loss
Start in her stomach.
It would take hold of her muscles and
Twist them around, wringing
The strength out of her.

Then the loss would move up
To her chest where it would
Catch her short of breath until
She couldn't release
The stale air inside of her.

It lingered in her throat, the loss,
Then in her face.
Her eyes were the last to try
To manage it.

Blinking down the misery
And the grief back to her gut,
She would
Consider herself in control.

But after while, there the suffering
Would start in her again.
The loss would never reach her brain.
So the widow never understood it.

On Staying Behind

You will be with me.
I will not let you go.
No.
No, I won't.
Well—
Yes, of course I will.
I would not bind
You
To this sodden life.
But in the same time,
In the same word,
In the same spirit,
I will not let you go.

I will see you
In the dishes
That I wash,
In the silver
That I store.

I will hear your
Voice in the sounds of the house,
In the rising up and the lying down.

I will hold you until
We are together
Yet again,
For a longer while
In another space,
At another time.

© 2011 Susan Patterson

We Are Just Visitors

Most likely you got a rear end slap
And responded with a loud outcry

Where am I?

If you think that first slap was harsh
Get ready for what's coming next
Be it short or a long stay

It doesn't matter...

In the end
Most likely
You will complain

Not enough time!

To be or not to be
Is not a question

It's a choice...

The purpose of our visit
To this tiny blue planet
Is very simple

Follow the rules of the Universe!

Leave a legacy
To better humankind
Because Karma is a bitch
And that rear end slap
May just be a reminder

That you are back again

162

Not the End of the Road

Below the sand
way deep in the darkness
the flowers are blooming
in the desert garden

www.ingramcontent.com/pod-product-compliance
Lightning Source LLC
Chambersburg PA
CBHW070659130626
46553CB00005B/1773